NAVIGATING NARCISSISM:

UNDERSTANDING AND COPING WITH NARCISSIST PERSONALITIES

Table of Contents

Understanding Narcissism and Coping with Narcissistic Personalities

In the complex landscape of human personalities and relationships, narcissism stands as a formidable force, shaping interactions and leaving its mark on those involved. Whether you've encountered a self-absorbed coworker, a demanding boss, an emotionally distant partner, or a manipulative family member, you may have questioned the nature of their behavior. What drives their insatiable need for admiration and their difficulty in empathizing with others? How do you navigate relationships with individuals who exhibit narcissistic traits? These are questions we will explore in this book, "Navigating Narcissism: Understanding and Coping with Narcissistic Personalities."

Defining Narcissism and Its Impact on Relationships

Narcissism, at its core, is a complex personality trait characterized by a heightened sense of self-importance, an excessive need for attention and admiration, and a lack of empathy for others. It is a term derived from Greek mythology, where Narcissus, a youth of unparalleled beauty, fell in love with his own reflection. In modern psychology, narcissism encompasses a spectrum, from healthy self-esteem to pathological narcissistic personality disorder (NPD). Narcissistic traits can be observed in varying degrees in many individuals, but when they become excessive and disruptive, they can have a profound impact on relationships.

Narcissism's impact on relationships is far-reaching. It can erode trust, create emotional turmoil, and leave loved ones feeling devalued and unheard. Those with narcissistic traits often struggle to establish meaningful connections, as their focus on self-validation can overshadow the needs and feelings of others. Understanding the dynamics of narcissistic behavior is essential, as it can empower you to navigate these relationships with greater clarity and resilience.

The Purpose of This Book

The purpose of "Navigating Narcissism" is to shed light on the enigmatic world of narcissistic personalities and provide you with the knowledge, strategies, and tools to effectively cope with them. This book is not intended to pathologize or stigmatize individuals with narcissistic traits. Rather, it seeks to offer insights into the nature of narcissism and the impact it has on those involved with narcissistic individuals. By fostering understanding and compassion, we can build healthier and more fulfilling relationships.

The Importance of Understanding and Managing Narcissistic Traits in Others

Why is it crucial to understand and manage narcissistic traits in others? The answer lies in the power of knowledge and self-preservation. When you can recognize narcissistic behaviors and their underlying motivations, you are better equipped to set boundaries, protect your emotional well-being, and engage in healthier interactions.

This knowledge can empower you to maintain your self-esteem and assert your needs, even in the face of challenging personalities.

By the end of this journey through the intricacies of narcissism, you will have a deeper understanding of what drives narcissistic behaviors and, more importantly, how to navigate them with grace, self-assurance, and empathy. You will discover that while narcissistic personalities may present complex challenges, they also offer opportunities for personal growth and transformation. By empowering yourself with the knowledge contained within these pages, you can turn what may seem like an insurmountable obstacle into a path of self-discovery and resilience.

So, let us embark on this exploration of narcissism, delve into the complexities of human nature, and find ways to navigate the intricate web of relationships affected by narcissistic traits. Together, we will work to understand, cope with, and ultimately thrive in the presence of narcissistic personalities.

Narcissism is a term that has found its way into everyday conversation, often used casually to describe someone who seems self-absorbed or excessively focused on their own needs and desires. But beneath this surface understanding lies a far more complex and nuanced psychological trait. In this chapter, we will delve deeper into the heart of narcissism, exploring its core characteristics and the spectrum of narcissistic traits that range from healthy self-esteem to Narcissistic Personality Disorder (NPD).

Defining Narcissism and Its Core Characteristics

At its core, narcissism is a personality trait marked by an excessive preoccupation with oneself and a lack of empathy for others. The term "narcissism" originates from Greek mythology, where Narcissus, a young man of extraordinary beauty, fell in love with his own reflection in a pool of water. In psychology, narcissism encompasses a wide array of behaviors, attitudes, and personality traits, but it is generally characterized by the following core features:

- Grandiosity: Narcissists often exhibit an inflated sense of self-importance and a belief that they are superior to others. They may exaggerate their achievements and talents, seeking constant admiration and validation from those around them.
- Need for Admiration: One of the hallmark characteristics of narcissism is an insatiable need for attention and admiration. Narcissists crave constant praise and affirmation, often fishing for compliments

or engaging in self-promotion.

- Lack of Empathy: A striking feature of narcissism is the inability to empathize with others. Narcissists have difficulty understanding or caring about the feelings and needs of those around them. They may exploit or manipulate others to achieve their own goals.

- Fantasies of Success, Power, or Beauty: Narcissists frequently engage in grandiose fantasies of unlimited success, power, beauty, or ideal love. These fantasies can serve as a way to escape feelings of inadequacy.

- Fragile Self-Esteem: Paradoxically, beneath the veneer of grandiosity, many narcissists have a fragile self-esteem. Criticism or perceived threats to their self-worth can trigger intense defensiveness and anger.

The Spectrum of Narcissistic Traits

It's important to recognize that narcissism exists on a spectrum, with varying degrees of intensity. At one end of the spectrum, we find individuals with healthy self-esteem, while at the other, we encounter those with Narcissistic Personality Disorder (NPD). Let's take a closer look at this spectrum:

- Healthy Self-Esteem: At the lowest end of the narcissism spectrum, we have individuals with healthy self-esteem. They possess a balanced sense of self-worth, allowing them to feel confident, competent, and valued without the need for excessive validation from others. These individuals can empathize with others and maintain healthy relationships.

- Narcissistic Traits: Moving along the spectrum, we encounter individuals who display narcissistic traits without necessarily meeting the criteria for NPD. These traits may include occasional self-centeredness, a desire for recognition, and a need for validation. While these individuals can be challenging to deal with, they still have the capacity for empathy and self-reflection.

- Narcissistic Personality Disorder (NPD): At the extreme end of the spectrum lies Narcissistic Personality Disorder (NPD). Individuals with NPD exhibit a pervasive pattern of grandiosity, a constant need for admiration, and a lack of empathy that significantly impairs their relationships and functioning in various aspects of life. NPD is a clinical diagnosis that requires the guidance of a mental health professional for assessment and treatment.

Understanding where an individual falls on this spectrum is crucial for effectively navigating relationships with them. It enables us to tailor our approach and expectations, whether that involves fostering healthy communication, setting boundaries, or seeking professional help when necessary.

<u>Chapter 2: The Origins of Narcissism</u>

Narcissism, with its intricate tapestry of behaviors and traits, is a complex phenomenon that doesn't arise in a vacuum. It has roots and origins, often stemming from a combination of various factors. In this chapter, we will delve into the potential causes and development of narcissistic traits, exploring the roles of genetics, upbringing, and environmental factors in shaping the narcissistic personality.

The Multifaceted Development of Narcissistic Traits

Narcissism doesn't have a singular, easily traceable cause. Instead, it is the product of a complex interplay of multiple factors. Understanding these factors can provide insight into the development of narcissistic traits in individuals. While the field of psychology continues to explore the origins of narcissism, several key elements have emerged as significant contributors:

Genetic Factors: Research suggests that genetics play a role in the development of narcissistic traits. Studies have identified a hereditary component, indicating that narcissism may run in families. Certain genetic variations may make some individuals more susceptible to developing narcissistic traits than others.

Upbringing and Parental Influence: The family environment, particularly parental influence, is a pivotal factor in the development of narcissism. Children are highly impressionable, and the behaviors and attitudes of their caregivers can significantly impact their self-esteem, self-worth, and sense of entitlement.

Overindulgent Parenting: Children raised by overly permissive or indulgent parents may develop narcissistic traits. Excessive praise, overvaluation, and the absence of consistent discipline can foster an exaggerated sense of entitlement.

Neglect or Abuse: On the flip side, children who experience neglect, emotional abuse, or inconsistent parenting may develop narcissistic traits as a defence mechanism to shield themselves from emotional pain.

Environmental Factors: Beyond the family, the broader environment also plays a role in nurturing narcissistic traits. Factors such as peer interactions, social media, and cultural values can contribute to the development of narcissism. For example, a society that emphasizes individual achievement, celebrity culture, and the pursuit of fame can amplify narcissistic tendencies.

Early Life Experiences: Traumatic or adverse childhood experiences, such as loss, abandonment, or humiliation, can be catalysts for narcissistic traits. These experiences may lead individuals to develop mechanisms of self-defence and self-enhancement.

Personality Development: Personality theories, such as Erikson's stages of psychosocial development, suggest that narcissistic traits can emerge during the "identity vs. role confusion" stage in adolescence. The formation of identity and self-concept during this critical period can shape narcissistic tendencies.

Coping Mechanisms: In some cases, narcissistic traits may be adaptive coping mechanisms in response to emotional wounds or feelings of inferiority. Individuals who have experienced rejection or a lack of love may use narcissism as a way to protect themselves from further emotional harm.

It's essential to note that not everyone who experiences these factors will develop narcissistic traits, and not all narcissistic traits lead to Narcissistic Personality Disorder (NPD). Many individuals exhibit narcissistic traits without crossing the threshold into a diagnosable personality disorder.

Understanding the origins of narcissism is a complex and ongoing endeavor. While we may identify contributing factors, the development of narcissistic traits remains a subject of much debate and research within the field of psychology.

Throughout history, there have been notable figures whose behaviors and characteristics align with what we now understand as narcissism. These individuals often exhibited a mix of qualities that could be perceived as both good and bad, reflecting the complexity of narcissistic traits.

1. **Alexander the Great:** One of history's most famous conquerors, Alexander the Great, is often cited as exhibiting narcissistic tendencies. His ambition, charisma, and confidence propelled him to great heights of conquest, expanding his empire across vast territories. However, his relentless pursuit of power and glory, coupled with a sense of entitlement and grandiosity, led to destructive wars and a legacy of hubris. While his leadership inspired awe and admiration, it also brought suffering and devastation to countless people.

2. **Napoleon Bonaparte:** Another iconic historical figure known for his narcissistic traits is Napoleon Bonaparte. His unparalleled ambition, strategic brilliance, and charisma enabled him to rise from humble origins to become Emperor of France. Napoleon's confidence and charisma captivated the masses, earning him a devoted following and reshaping the political landscape of Europe. However, his insatiable desire for conquest, coupled with a lack of empathy and disregard for human life, led to widespread suffering and upheaval. His downfall, marked by defeat and exile, underscored the consequences of unchecked narcissism.

3. **Cleopatra VII:** Cleopatra VII, the last active ruler of the Ptolemaic Kingdom of Egypt, is often depicted as a figure of immense beauty, intelligence, and charm. Her ability to captivate powerful men, including Julius Caesar and Mark Antony, speaks to her magnetic personality and strategic acumen. Cleopatra's ambition and cunning enabled her to maintain her grip on power in a male-dominated world, wielding influence and shaping the course of history. However, her manipulative tendencies and willingness to exploit others for personal gain also highlight the darker aspects of narcissism, leading to betrayal and tragedy.

Qualities of Historical Narcissists:

Historical narcissists exhibited a range of qualities, both positive and negative, that contributed to their influence and impact on the world:

1. **Charisma and Leadership:** Narcissistic individuals often possess charisma and magnetism that draw others to them. Historical narcissists such as Alexander the Great and Napoleon Bonaparte were able to inspire loyalty and devotion among their followers, rallying armies and shaping the course of history through their leadership.

2. **Ambition and Vision:** Narcissists are driven by an insatiable desire for success and recognition, often pursuing ambitious goals with relentless determination. Figures like Alexander the Great and Cleopatra VII demonstrated a vision for greatness, striving to leave their mark on the world through conquest, innovation, or political maneuvering.

3. **Manipulation and Deception:** Narcissists are skilled manipulators who use charm, persuasion, and deception to achieve their objectives. Historical narcissists such as Cleopatra VII were adept at manipulating powerful men to serve their own interests, employing seduction, flattery, and intrigue to maintain their grip on power.

4. **Hubris and Arrogance:** Narcissists often exhibit a sense of grandiosity and entitlement that can lead to hubris and overconfidence. Figures like Napoleon Bonaparte famously underestimated their opponents and overestimated their own abilities, leading to costly mistakes and eventual downfall.

5. **Lack of Empathy:** One of the defining characteristics of narcissism is a lack of empathy and concern for others' feelings. Historical narcissists often prioritized their own ambitions and desires above the well-being of others, leading to exploitation, betrayal, and suffering.

The historical examples of narcissistic individuals offer valuable insights into the origins and manifestations of narcissism throughout human history. While figures like Alexander the Great, Napoleon Bonaparte, and Cleopatra VII exhibited qualities that propelled them to greatness, their narcissistic traits also brought about destruction, suffering, and downfall. By examining the complexities of historical narcissists, we can better understand the enduring influence of narcissism on individuals and societies across time.

Recognizing narcissistic behavior is a crucial first step in navigating relationships with individuals who exhibit narcissistic traits. By understanding the telltale signs and patterns associated with narcissism, you can better prepare yourself for the challenges that may arise. In this chapter, we'll provide insights and examples of narcissistic behaviors and attitudes, empowering you to identify these traits in the people you interact with.

Insights into Narcissistic Behaviors and Attitudes

Narcissistic behaviors and attitudes manifest in various ways, each offering unique insights into the mind of a narcissist. While not every individual will display all these traits, a combination of these characteristics often defines narcissistic personalities:

- Exaggerated Self-Importance: Narcissists often hold an inflated view of themselves and their abilities. They may boast about their accomplishments, seek constant admiration, and believe they are unique or special.
- Need for Constant Admiration: One of the most distinctive signs of narcissism is the unending need for admiration. Narcissists expect others to affirm their greatness, often fishing for compliments or becoming angry when they don't receive the praise they desire.
- Lack of Empathy: Empathy, the ability to understand and share the feelings of others, is a hallmark trait that narcissists typically lack. They may be dismissive of others' emotions and struggle to see situations from someone else's perspective.

- Manipulation and Exploitation: Narcissists may use others to achieve their goals without regard for their feelings or well-being. They might manipulate situations, spread misinformation, or engage in emotional and psychological manipulation to maintain control.

- Sense of Entitlement: Narcissists often have a strong sense of entitlement. They believe that the rules don't apply to them and may become angry or indignant when they don't receive preferential treatment.

- Fragile Self-Esteem: Despite their outward grandiosity, many narcissists have fragile self-esteem. Criticism, even when constructive, can be met with defensiveness, anger, or a deep sense of wounded pride.

- Envy and Competition: Narcissists may harbour intense envy towards those they perceive as superior or more successful. They often engage in competitive behaviors to prove their worth and superiority.

- Superficial Relationships: Narcissists often struggle to maintain deep, meaningful connections. Their relationships tend to be superficial and transactional, driven by the need for validation rather than genuine connection.

Examples of Narcissistic Behaviors

To help you recognize narcissistic traits more easily, let's consider some common examples of narcissistic behaviors and attitudes:

Example 1: Constant Self-Promotion: A coworker who consistently talks about their achievements and seeks praise, yet rarely acknowledges the contributions of others, may display narcissistic traits.

Example 2: Lack of Empathy: A friend who shows little concern for your struggles or emotions, always redirecting the conversation back to themselves, may exhibit narcissistic behavior.

Example 3: Manipulative Tactics: A family member who uses guilt trips, emotional manipulation, or deception to get their way may have narcissistic tendencies.

Example 4: Entitlement: A romantic partner who believes they deserve preferential treatment and becomes angry when their expectations aren't met may display narcissistic traits.

Example 5: Competitive Streak: A colleague who constantly tries to outdo you or others, often displaying jealousy when others receive recognition, might have narcissistic tendencies.

Identifying Narcissistic Traits in People You Interact With

Identifying narcissistic traits in people you interact with is a valuable skill, but it's important to approach this process with caution and empathy. Narcissistic behavior may vary in intensity, and individuals may exhibit some traits without fitting a complete profile of Narcissistic Personality Disorder (NPD).

To help you recognize narcissistic traits in those around you, consider the following:

Observation: Pay attention to recurring patterns of behavior, especially in situations where narcissistic traits tend to emerge, such as conflicts or discussions about success and recognition.

Trust Your Instincts: If you consistently feel undervalued, manipulated, or dismissed in a relationship, trust your instincts and investigate further.

Consult with Trusted Friends: Discuss your observations and experiences with trusted friends or family members. They may offer an outside perspective on the dynamics of the relationship.

Seek Professional Guidance: If you suspect that someone's narcissistic traits are causing significant harm or distress in your life, consider consulting with a mental health professional who can provide guidance and support.

Recognizing narcissistic behavior is an essential step in navigating relationships with individuals who exhibit these traits. It allows you to approach these relationships with greater awareness, set boundaries, and make informed decisions about how to proceed.

<u>Chapter 4: The Impact of Narcissism on Relationships</u>

Narcissistic traits have a profound and far-reaching impact on various types of relationships, often leaving a trail of emotional turmoil and psychological distress. In this chapter, we will explore how narcissistic traits affect romantic, familial, and professional relationships, while also delving into the emotional and psychological toll experienced by those dealing with narcissistic individuals.

Narcissism's Influence on Different Types of Relationships

1. Romantic Relationships:

Romantic relationships with narcissistic partners can be tumultuous and emotionally draining. Common dynamics in such relationships include:

Love-Bombing: Narcissists often engage in "love-bombing" at the start of the relationship, showering their partner with affection and attention. This intense focus can make their partner feel special and cherished. However, it's often followed by devaluation as the narcissist's interest wanes, leaving their partner feeling unimportant and rejected.

Emotional Manipulation: Narcissistic partners may use emotional manipulation to control their significant other. Gaslighting, guilt-tripping, and silent treatment are all tactics employed to assert dominance and maintain power in the relationship.

Lack of Empathy: Narcissists' inability to empathize can lead to a lack of emotional support when their partner faces challenges or difficult emotions. This emotional neglect can create a sense of isolation and loneliness.

Familial Relationships:
Narcissistic traits within families can disrupt bonds and create a hostile environment. Common family dynamics include:

- Parental Narcissism: A narcissistic parent may prioritize their own needs and desires over those of their children. This can lead to feelings of inadequacy, neglect, and the development of low self-esteem in the child.
- Sibling Rivalry: In families with narcissistic dynamics, sibling rivalry is often heightened. The narcissistic individual may pit siblings against each other for their favor, leading to strained relationships between siblings.
- Emotional Turmoil: Family members dealing with a narcissistic parent or sibling may experience ongoing emotional turmoil, guilt, and a sense of obligation to meet the narcissist's demands.

Professional Relationships:

Narcissistic traits in the workplace can create a challenging environment for colleagues and subordinates. Key dynamics include:

- Power Struggles: Narcissistic superiors may engage in power struggles, seeking to dominate or undermine subordinates. This behavior can lead to workplace conflict and decreased job satisfaction.

Credit Hoarding: Narcissistic colleagues may be reluctant to share credit for accomplishments and may undermine the efforts of others to maintain their own position in the spotlight.

Lack of Accountability: Narcissistic individuals in professional settings often deflect blame and responsibility onto others. This lack of accountability can harm teamwork and overall organizational performance.

The Emotional and Psychological Toll

Dealing with narcissistic individuals in any type of relationship can exact a heavy emotional and psychological toll. The impacts can be varied and profound, including:

- Low Self-Esteem: Constant criticism, devaluation, and emotional manipulation can erode the self-esteem and self-worth of those interacting with narcissistic individuals.
- Anxiety and Depression: The ongoing turmoil and unpredictability in relationships with narcissists can lead to anxiety and depression as individuals grapple with constant stress and emotional turmoil.
- Isolation: Narcissists' inability to empathize can leave their victims feeling isolated and emotionally abandoned, resulting in a sense of loneliness and despair.
- Self-Doubt: Manipulative tactics and gaslighting can instill self-doubt in those interacting with narcissistic individuals, making them question their own perceptions and judgments.

- Emotional Exhaustion: The constant need for validation and praise, coupled with the emotional ups and downs of such relationships, can lead to emotional exhaustion and burnout.

The emotional and psychological impact of dealing with narcissistic individuals is not to be underestimated. It's important to recognize the toll that these relationships can take on your well-being and mental health.

Relationships involving narcissistic individuals can be tumultuous and emotionally draining. Understanding the dynamics at play is crucial for navigating these challenging waters. In this chapter, we delve into the various ways narcissism impacts relationships and how narcissists react to different behaviors within these relationships.

Emotional Manipulation:

- Narcissists are adept at manipulating emotions to serve their own needs. They often employ tactics such as gaslighting, where they deny or distort reality to make their partner doubt their perceptions. This can lead to confusion and self-doubt in the partner, ultimately eroding trust and intimacy in the relationship.
- Reaction: When confronted about their manipulative behavior, narcissists may become defensive and turn the blame back on their partner. They might dismiss their partner's concerns as irrational or overreactive, further exacerbating feelings of inadequacy and frustration.

Lack of Empathy:

- One of the hallmark traits of narcissism is a profound lack of empathy. Narcissists struggle to understand or connect with their partner's emotions, often prioritizing their own needs and desires above all else. This can leave their partner feeling neglected and emotionally unfulfilled.
- Reaction: When faced with their partner's emotional needs, narcissists may trivialize or dismiss them altogether. They might belittle their partner's feelings, viewing them as insignificant compared to their own. Alternatively, they may become enraged or defensive, viewing any attempt to address their lack of empathy as an attack on their character.

Need for Validation:

- Narcissists have an insatiable need for validation and admiration from others. They crave constant praise and attention to bolster their fragile sense of self-worth. In relationships, this can manifest as an overwhelming demand for affirmation and reassurance from their partner.
- Reaction: When their partner fails to meet their need for validation, narcissists may resort to manipulation or coercion to elicit the desired response. They may become sulky or withdrawn, employing tactics such as the silent treatment to punish their partner for not meeting their expectations. Alternatively, they may seek validation elsewhere, engaging in extramarital affairs or seeking attention from other sources.

Sense of Entitlement:

- Narcissists often possess an inflated sense of entitlement, believing that they are inherently deserving of special treatment and privileges. This can lead to a sense of entitlement within the relationship, where the narcissist expects their partner to cater to their every whim without question.
- Reaction: When their sense of entitlement is challenged, narcissists may react with indignation or rage. They may lash out at their partner, accusing them of being selfish or ungrateful for not meeting their needs. Alternatively, they may resort to manipulation or coercion to get their way, using tactics such as guilt-tripping or emotional blackmail.

The Positive Aspects of Narcissism

While narcissism is often associated with negative traits such as selfishness, manipulation, and a lack of empathy, it's essential to acknowledge that there can be positive aspects to narcissistic personality traits. In certain contexts, narcissism can manifest as confidence, ambition, and charisma, which can be beneficial in various aspects of life and relationships.

1. **Confidence and Self-Assurance:** Narcissistic individuals often possess a strong sense of confidence and self-assurance that enables them to pursue their goals with determination and resilience. This confidence can be infectious, inspiring others to believe in themselves and their abilities. In professional settings, narcissistic traits such as self-confidence and assertiveness can lead to success in leadership roles, entrepreneurship, and public speaking. Individuals with healthy narcissism are not afraid to take risks or assert themselves, leading to innovation and growth in their endeavors.

2. **Ambition and Achievement:** Narcissistic traits such as ambition and a desire for recognition can drive individuals to achieve great things in their careers and personal lives. The relentless pursuit of success and validation can lead to innovation, creativity, and a willingness to push boundaries.

In competitive fields such as business, sports, and entertainment, narcissistic individuals may excel due to their drive to outperform others and prove their worth. Their ambition can inspire others to set and pursue their own goals, creating a culture of achievement and excellence.

3. **Charisma and Influence:** Narcissistic individuals often possess charisma and charm that draw others to them and inspire admiration and loyalty. Their magnetic personality and confidence can make them effective leaders, influencers, and motivators. In social settings, narcissistic traits such as charm and wit can make interactions enjoyable and engaging, leading to the formation of meaningful connections and friendships. People are naturally drawn to individuals who exude confidence and charisma, making narcissists adept at networking and building social capital.

4. **Resilience and Adaptability:** Narcissistic individuals are often resilient in the face of adversity, possessing a strong belief in their own abilities to overcome challenges and setbacks. Their confidence and optimism can help them bounce back from failures and setbacks, turning obstacles into opportunities for growth and learning. In relationships, narcissistic traits such as resilience and adaptability can help individuals navigate difficult circumstances and maintain a sense of optimism and hope for the future.

5. **Creativity and Innovation:** Narcissistic individuals are often creative and innovative thinkers who are unafraid to challenge conventions and explore new ideas. Their confidence in their own abilities and willingness to take risks can lead to breakthroughs in art, science, technology, and other fields. Narcissistic traits such as a desire for recognition and admiration can drive individuals to pursue unconventional paths and make bold choices that push the boundaries of what is possible. Their willingness to take risks and think outside the box can lead to discoveries and advancements that benefit society as a whole.

While narcissism is often associated with negative traits, it's essential to recognize that there can be positive aspects to narcissistic personality traits as well. Confidence, ambition, charisma, resilience, and creativity are all qualities that can lead to success and fulfillment in various aspects of life and relationships. By harnessing the positive aspects of narcissism while mitigating its negative effects, individuals can achieve their goals, inspire others, and make meaningful contributions to the world.

Chapter 5: Coping Strategies for Dealing with Narcissism

Coping with narcissistic behavior is no small feat, and it often requires a combination of strategies to protect yourself and maintain your emotional well-being. In this chapter, we will explore practical tips and strategies to help you manage and protect yourself from the effects of narcissistic behavior. We will delve into the importance of setting boundaries, practicing self-care, and building emotional resilience.

Practical Tips and Strategies for Coping

Set Clear Boundaries: Establishing and maintaining boundaries is paramount when dealing with narcissistic individuals. Communicate your limits, and be firm in enforcing them. Recognize that narcissists may push back against your boundaries, but consistency is key.

Avoid Escalation: Narcissists thrive on conflict and power struggles. Avoid getting drawn into unnecessary arguments or confrontations. Responding calmly and rationally can prevent escalation.

Limit Contact: When possible, reduce contact with the narcissistic individual. This can provide you with much-needed emotional distance and relief from the constant stress of the relationship.

Practice Active Listening: In conversations with the narcissist, actively listen and validate their feelings, even if you don't agree with their perspective. This can help diffuse potential conflicts.

Maintain a Support Network: Seek support from friends, family, or support groups. Sharing your experiences with empathetic individuals can offer emotional relief and help you feel less isolated.

Setting and Maintaining Boundaries

Setting boundaries is a crucial aspect of coping with narcissistic behavior. Here are some strategies to help you establish and maintain healthy boundaries:

- Define Your Boundaries: Clearly identify the behaviors or actions that are unacceptable to you. Communicate these boundaries assertively but not aggressively.
- Stay Consistent: Once you've set boundaries, it's essential to maintain them consistently. Narcissistic individuals may test your limits, so be unwavering in enforcing your boundaries.
- Protect Your Time: Guard your time and energy. It's perfectly acceptable to say no to additional demands or obligations that infringe on your well-being.
- Seek Professional Guidance: Consider consulting with a therapist or counselor who can help you establish and maintain boundaries effectively.

Self-Care Strategies

Self-care is essential when dealing with narcissistic behavior. It allows you to prioritize your well-being and maintain your emotional health. Here are some self-care strategies to consider:

Set Aside "Me" Time: Dedicate time for activities that bring you joy and relaxation. This can be anything from reading, practicing a hobby, or taking a walk in nature.

Prioritize Physical Health: Regular exercise, a balanced diet, and sufficient sleep are vital for maintaining your physical and emotional well-being.

Practice Mindfulness and Stress Reduction: Engage in mindfulness techniques, meditation, or deep breathing exercises to manage stress and maintain emotional balance.

Seek Professional Help: If you find that your emotional well-being is significantly impacted, consider therapy or counseling to help you cope with the emotional toll of dealing with a narcissistic individual.

Building Emotional Resilience

Emotional resilience is the ability to bounce back from adversity and maintain your well-being. When dealing with narcissistic individuals, developing emotional resilience is key. Here's how you can work on building this strength:

Develop a Support System: Lean on friends and family for emotional support. Having a strong support network can bolster your resilience.

Reframe Negative Thoughts: Practice reframing negative thoughts into more positive and realistic ones. This can help you maintain a more balanced perspective.

Focus on What You Can Control: Recognize that you can't change the narcissistic individual, but you can control your reactions and boundaries.

Stay True to Your Values: Clarify your values and what's most important to you. Staying aligned with your core values can provide a sense of purpose and resilience.

Coping with narcissistic behavior is a challenging journey, but it's possible to protect your well-being and maintain your emotional health. By setting boundaries, prioritizing self-care, and building emotional resilience, you can navigate these relationships with greater confidence and resilience.

Navigating relationships with narcissistic individuals can be mentally and emotionally taxing, but implementing effective coping strategies can help mitigate the impact of their behavior. Beyond setting boundaries, practicing self-care, and building emotional resilience, there are additional tactics individuals can employ to navigate these challenging dynamics.

1. **Maintain Realistic Expectations:** It's essential to recognize that narcissists are unlikely to change their behavior fundamentally. Accepting this reality can help individuals manage their expectations within the relationship. Instead of hoping for genuine empathy or understanding from the narcissist, focus on protecting your own well-being and establishing boundaries to minimize harm.

2. **Limit Emotional Investment:** Recognize that investing too much emotional energy into the relationship with a narcissist may lead to disappointment and frustration. Instead of expecting reciprocity or validation from the narcissist, channel your emotional energy into fulfilling activities and relationships outside of the narcissistic dynamic. Cultivate a support network of friends, family, or therapists who can provide validation and empathy outside of the relationship.

3. **Practice Detachment:** Emotional detachment can be a valuable coping mechanism when dealing with narcissists. Instead of becoming enmeshed in their drama or manipulation, maintain a sense of detachment and perspective.

Remind yourself that the narcissist's behavior is a reflection of their own insecurities and issues, rather than a reflection of your worth or value as a person. Focus on maintaining your own emotional equilibrium and not allowing the narcissist to dictate your emotional state.

4. **Develop Assertiveness Skills:** Assertiveness is crucial when setting and enforcing boundaries with narcissists. Practice clear and direct communication, expressing your needs and boundaries assertively without aggression or hostility. Use "I" statements to express your feelings and preferences, and be prepared to reinforce your boundaries with consequences if they are violated. For example, if the narcissist continues to engage in manipulative behavior despite your boundaries, you may need to limit contact or seek support from a therapist or mediator.

5. **Focus on Self-Validation:** In relationships with narcissists, external validation may be scarce or unreliable. Therefore, it's essential to cultivate self-validation and self-worth internally. Practice affirming yourself and recognizing your own strengths and accomplishments, independent of external validation from the narcissist. Engage in activities that bring you joy and fulfillment, bolstering your self-esteem and confidence from within.

6. **Seek Professional Support:** Dealing with narcissistic individuals can be emotionally draining and complex, and seeking support from a therapist or counselor can be invaluable.

A trained professional can provide validation, perspective, and coping strategies tailored to your specific situation. Therapy can also serve as a safe space to process your emotions, explore patterns in your relationships, and develop healthier coping mechanisms.

7. **Set Realistic Boundaries:** While setting boundaries is crucial, it's also essential to set boundaries that are realistic and enforceable within the context of the relationship. Avoid setting boundaries that rely on the narcissist changing their behavior or meeting unrealistic expectations. Instead, focus on setting boundaries that prioritize your emotional well-being and protect you from harm. Be prepared to enforce these boundaries consistently, even in the face of resistance or manipulation from the narcissist.

8. **Practice Self-Compassion:** Dealing with a narcissistic partner can be emotionally taxing and may lead to feelings of self-doubt, guilt, or shame. It's essential to practice self-compassion and kindness towards yourself during these challenging times. Remind yourself that you are not responsible for the narcissist's behavior, and you deserve compassion and understanding just as much as anyone else. Be gentle with yourself and prioritize self-care activities that nourish your mind, body, and soul.

Incorporating these coping strategies into your daily life can help you navigate relationships with narcissistic individuals more effectively, protect your emotional well-being, and maintain a sense of agency and control within the relationship.

Remember that while you may not be able to change the narcissist's behavior, you have the power to prioritize your own needs and boundaries, cultivate healthy relationships outside of the narcissistic dynamic, and ultimately thrive despite the challenges you may face.

Chapter 6: Communicating with a Narcissist

Effective communication with narcissistic individuals can be challenging, but it's essential for maintaining relationships and reducing conflicts. In this chapter, we will provide guidance on how to communicate with narcissistic individuals and discuss techniques for managing conflicts and minimizing confrontation.

Effective Communication with Narcissistic Individuals

Maintain Calm and Composure: When communicating with a narcissistic individual, it's crucial to remain calm and composed. Emotional reactions can escalate conflicts. Try to keep your emotions in check, even when faced with provocation.

Use "I" Statements: Frame your statements using "I" rather than "you" to express your feelings and needs. For example, say, "I feel hurt when..." instead of "You always do..."

Be Specific: When addressing concerns, provide specific examples or instances that illustrate your point. Concrete examples make it harder for the narcissistic individual to dismiss your concerns as vague or unfounded.

Active Listening: Show that you're actively listening by making eye contact, nodding, and providing verbal acknowledgments. This can help prevent the narcissist from feeling ignored or invalidated.

Stay Solution-Focused: While discussing problems or conflicts, keep the conversation focused on finding solutions. This approach may encourage the narcissistic individual to engage constructively rather than defensively.

Techniques for Managing Conflicts

1. **Choose Your Battles:** Not every issue is worth confronting a narcissistic individual about. Consider whether the issue is critical and if addressing it is likely to result in a positive change. Sometimes, it's best to let minor issues go.
2. **Use Diplomacy:** Practice diplomacy and tact when discussing sensitive topics. Avoid confrontational language and use diplomacy to convey your point.
3. **Set Realistic Expectations:** Understand that narcissistic individuals may not be willing or capable of substantial change. Set realistic expectations for what you can achieve through communication.
4. **Pick the Right Time and Place:** Timing and environment matter. Choose a time and place where both parties can speak without interruptions or distractions. This can help maintain a focused and respectful conversation.
5. **Provide Positive Reinforcement:** When the narcissistic individual exhibits positive behavior, acknowledge and reinforce it. This can encourage them to repeat those behaviors.

Minimizing Confrontation

Avoid Triggering Language: Pay attention to language that may trigger defensive reactions. Steer clear of blame, accusations, and inflammatory statements.

Use Neutral Tone and Body Language: Maintain a neutral and non-confrontational tone of voice and body language during discussions. Avoid aggressive postures or gestures.

Empathize with Their Perspective: Even if you disagree with the narcissistic individual, attempt to understand their perspective. This can help lower their guard and foster more constructive communication.

Offer Praise and Admiration: Narcissists respond well to praise and admiration. Offering genuine compliments can help create a more positive atmosphere and reduce tension.

Limit Exposure: If communication becomes consistently negative and harmful, consider limiting your exposure to the narcissistic individual. Reducing contact can be a form of self-preservation.

While communication with a narcissistic individual is undoubtedly challenging, it's not impossible. By using these strategies and techniques, you can navigate discussions more effectively and minimize confrontations. Keep in mind that it may take time to see significant changes in the dynamics of your relationship.

Communication with narcissists can be challenging due to their tendency to prioritize their own needs and desires over others'. In this chapter, we explore additional methods of communication with narcissists, as well as how they typically communicate with others.

1. **Validation and Empathy:** While narcissists struggle to provide validation and empathy to others, offering it to them can sometimes help facilitate communication. Acknowledging their feelings, even if you don't agree with them, can help prevent defensiveness and open the door to more constructive dialogue. For example, saying something like, "I understand that you're feeling frustrated right now," can help validate their emotions without necessarily condoning their behavior.

2. **Use Concrete Examples:** When addressing issues or conflicts with a narcissist, using concrete examples can be more effective than abstract concepts. Narcissists often struggle to grasp complex emotions or hypothetical scenarios, so providing specific instances of their behavior and its impact can help them understand your perspective more clearly. For instance, instead of saying, "You always make me feel unimportant," you could say, "When you cancel plans at the last minute without explanation, it makes me feel like my time isn't valued."

3. **Frame Communication in Terms of Their Self-Interest:** Narcissists are often driven by their own self-interest, so framing communication in terms of how it benefits them can be more persuasive.

Highlighting how addressing a particular issue or compromise aligns with their goals or desires can increase their motivation to engage constructively. For example, you might say, "If we can find a compromise on this issue, it will improve our relationship and create a more positive environment for both of us."

4. **Set Clear Expectations:** Clearly communicating your expectations and boundaries with narcissists is crucial for establishing mutual understanding and preventing misunderstandings. Be specific about what you need or expect from them in terms of behavior or communication, and be prepared to enforce these expectations consistently. Setting clear boundaries can help minimize conflicts and prevent manipulation or exploitation. For example, you might say, "I expect honesty and transparency in our communication, and if I feel like you're being deceitful, I will need to reevaluate our relationship."

How Narcissists Typically Communicate:

Narcissists often communicate in ways that prioritize their own needs and desires while disregarding or dismissing the feelings of others. Their communication style is often characterized by:

1. **Self-Aggrandizement:** Narcissists frequently engage in self-promotion and exaggeration to bolster their own self-image and elicit admiration from others. They may embellish their accomplishments, talents, or experiences to garner praise and validation, often at the expense of truthfulness or authenticity.

2. **Manipulation and Gaslighting:** Narcissists are skilled manipulators who use tactics such as gaslighting to control and undermine their partners. They may deny or distort reality, making their partner question their perceptions or sanity. For example, if confronted about their infidelity, a narcissist might accuse their partner of being paranoid or jealous, deflecting attention away from their own behavior.

3. **Lack of Empathy:** Narcissists struggle to empathize with others' emotions or perspectives, often dismissing or invalidating their feelings. They may minimize or trivialize their partner's concerns, viewing them as insignificant compared to their own needs. For example, if their partner expresses sadness or disappointment, a narcissist might respond with indifference or criticism, failing to offer comfort or support.

4. **Entitlement and Demands:** Narcissists have an inflated sense of entitlement and may make unreasonable demands of their partners. They expect special treatment and privileges without considering the needs or feelings of others. For example, a narcissist might insist on having their partner's undivided attention at all times, becoming enraged if their needs are not immediately met.

Communicating with a narcissist requires patience, assertiveness, and a deep understanding of their communication style and motivations. By employing strategies such as validation, concrete examples, framing communication in terms of their self-interest, and setting clear expectations, individuals can navigate interactions with narcissists more effectively while minimizing conflict and manipulation.

However, it's essential to recognize that effective communication with a narcissist may still be limited, and seeking support from a therapist or counselor can be invaluable for navigating these challenging dynamics.

Navigating a relationship with a narcissistic individual can be incredibly challenging. In some cases, it may become clear that professional help is needed to address the issues at hand. In this chapter, we will explain when and how to encourage a narcissistic individual to seek therapy or counseling. We'll also discuss the potential benefits of therapy for both the narcissist and those affected by their behavior.

When to Encourage a Narcissistic Individual to Seek Therapy

Encouraging a narcissistic individual to seek therapy is a delicate process that requires careful consideration. While you can't force someone to pursue therapy, there are situations in which it may be appropriate to suggest it:

Dangerous Behavior: If the narcissistic individual's behavior is putting themselves or others at risk, such as through substance abuse, self-harm, or aggressive actions, therapy may be a necessary intervention.

Severe Relationship Strain: When the relationship is on the brink of collapse due to constant conflicts and emotional distress, suggesting therapy may be a last-ditch effort to salvage the relationship.

Loss of Employment or Stability: If the narcissistic individual's behavior is causing significant problems in their professional life, therapy may help them develop healthier coping strategies and interpersonal skills.

Personal Desire for Change: In some cases, the narcissistic individual may express a desire to change or seek therapy themselves. This presents a more favorable opportunity for intervention.

How to Encourage a Narcissistic Individual to Seek Therapy

Encouraging a narcissistic individual to seek therapy can be a sensitive and challenging process. Here are some guidelines to follow:

1. **Choose the Right Moment:** Wait for a moment when the narcissistic individual is relatively calm and open to discussion. Avoid bringing up the topic during a conflict.
2. **Express Concern:** Communicate your concerns about their well-being and the impact their behavior is having on your relationship. Use "I" statements to express your feelings.
3. **Suggest Therapy as an Option:** Present therapy as a potential solution rather than a demand. You can say, "I think therapy might help us work through our issues" or "I've heard that therapy can be beneficial for improving relationships."
4. **Offer Support:** Express your willingness to support them throughout the therapy process, whether that means helping them find a therapist, attending sessions together, or simply providing emotional support.
5. **Be Patient:** Understand that the decision to seek therapy may take time. Be patient and give the individual space to consider the idea.

Potential Benefits of Therapy for Narcissists and Those Affected by Their Behavior

Therapy can offer significant benefits for both the narcissistic individual and those impacted by their behavior:

For the Narcissistic Individual:

Increased Self-Awareness: Therapy can help the narcissist gain insight into their behavior and its impact on others. This self-awareness is a critical first step towards change.

Improved Interpersonal Skills: Therapy can teach the individual healthier ways of relating to others, enhancing their ability to build and maintain relationships.

Emotional Regulation: Narcissistic individuals often struggle with emotional regulation. Therapy can help them develop skills to manage and express their emotions more effectively.

Personal Growth: Therapy can facilitate personal growth and self-improvement, leading to a more fulfilling and balanced life.

For Those Affected by Narcissistic Behavior:

Validation and Support: Therapy provides a safe space to discuss the challenges and emotional toll of dealing with a narcissistic individual. It offers validation and support for those affected.

Coping Strategies: Therapists can teach coping strategies and communication skills to manage the impact of narcissistic behavior more effectively.

Boundary Setting: Therapy can help individuals establish and maintain healthy boundaries, reducing the emotional harm caused by the narcissist.

Emotional Healing: Therapy can aid in the process of emotional healing, helping individuals rebuild their self-esteem and regain a sense of self-worth.

While therapy can be beneficial, it's important to recognize that not all narcissistic individuals are willing to seek help or change their behavior. In such cases, it's vital to focus on your own well-being and consider whether maintaining the relationship is in your best interest. Therapy can provide you with guidance and support in making these decisions.

Healing and recovering from relationships with narcissistic individuals is a challenging journey, but it is one that is essential for regaining emotional well-being and building resilience. In this chapter, we will explore the process of healing and recovery and provide insights into how to build resilience and self-esteem in the aftermath of such relationships.

The Process of Healing and Recovery

Recovering from a relationship with a narcissistic individual is a process that takes time and self-compassion. Here's a step-by-step guide to help you on your journey:

Acknowledge Your Feelings: Start by recognizing and validating your emotions. Understand that it's normal to feel hurt, angry, and confused after dealing with a narcissistic individual. Give yourself permission to feel and express these emotions.

Set Boundaries: Reinforce the boundaries you've established. Ensure that you're safeguarding your well-being and reducing exposure to toxic behaviors.

Seek Support: Lean on your support network, whether it's friends, family, or a therapist. Sharing your experiences and emotions with others can be incredibly therapeutic.

Self-Reflection: Take time to reflect on the relationship and your role in it. This self-reflection can provide valuable insights into your own needs, boundaries, and personal growth.

Learn from the Experience: Consider what you've learned from the relationship with the narcissistic individual. How can this experience be a source of personal growth and wisdom?

Self-Care: Prioritize self-care, both physically and emotionally. Engage in activities that bring you joy, relaxation, and a sense of well-being.

Emotional Healing: Work on healing emotional wounds and rebuilding your self-esteem. Recognize that the narcissistic individual's behavior was not a reflection of your worth.

Acceptance: Accept that you cannot change the narcissistic individual. Understand that their behavior is not a reflection of your worth or value.

Forgiveness: Consider forgiving the narcissistic individual, not for their sake, but for your own. Letting go of anger and resentment can be a powerful step in your healing journey.

Building Resilience and Self-Esteem

Building resilience and self-esteem is a vital part of the healing process. Here are some strategies to help you on this path:

Self-Compassion: Practice self-compassion by treating yourself with the same kindness and understanding you would offer to a friend. Be gentle with yourself and acknowledge that you did the best you could in a challenging situation.

Positive Self-Talk: Challenge negative self-talk and replace it with positive, affirming statements. Remind yourself of your strengths and accomplishments.

Set Achievable Goals: Break down your personal goals into smaller, achievable steps. Celebrate your progress and successes along the way.

Mindfulness and Relaxation: Engage in mindfulness practices and relaxation techniques to reduce stress and stay grounded in the present moment.

Focus on Your Passions: Pursue activities and interests that bring you joy and fulfillment. Reconnecting with your passions can boost self-esteem and a sense of purpose.

Connect with Positive People: Surround yourself with positive, supportive individuals who uplift you and reinforce your self-worth.

Therapy and Counseling: Consider therapy or counseling to work through any residual emotional wounds and build resilience. A professional can offer valuable guidance and support.

Accept Imperfections: Embrace your imperfections and understand that they make you unique. Perfection is not a realistic or attainable standard.

Healing and recovery from relationships with narcissistic individuals can be a long and sometimes arduous journey, but it is a path to emotional growth and resilience. By practicing self-compassion, nurturing your self-esteem, and employing the strategies mentioned above, you can find your way back to a place of emotional well-being and build a brighter, more positive future.

<u>Chapter 9: Narcissism in the Workplace</u>

Narcissism in the workplace can present unique challenges and complexities. Dealing with narcissistic coworkers or superiors requires a delicate balance of assertiveness, diplomacy, and self-preservation. In this chapter, we will address the challenges of working with narcissistic individuals and offer strategies for navigating workplace dynamics when narcissism is a factor.

Challenges of Dealing with Narcissistic Coworkers or Superiors

Ego-Centric Behavior: Narcissistic individuals in the workplace often display ego-centric behavior, which can lead to arrogance, a lack of empathy, and a sense of entitlement.

Credit Hoarding: Narcissistic coworkers or superiors may take credit for the work of others or undermine the contributions of their colleagues.

Power Struggles: Narcissistic individuals may engage in power struggles, seeking to dominate or undermine their coworkers or subordinates.

Lack of Accountability: Narcissistic coworkers often deflect blame and responsibility, potentially leading to workplace conflict and a decrease in job satisfaction.

Inconsistent Praise: Narcissists may offer praise or recognition inconsistently, using it as a tool for control rather than genuine acknowledgment.

Strategies for Navigating Workplace Dynamics

Navigating workplace dynamics with narcissistic individuals requires a combination of strategies to protect your well-being and maintain professionalism. Here are some strategies to consider:

Set Clear Boundaries: Establish and maintain clear boundaries in the workplace. Clearly define your role and responsibilities, and communicate your boundaries assertively but not aggressively.

Document Your Work: Keep records of your contributions and achievements. This documentation can be valuable in situations where credit hoarding or false accusations become issues.

Avoid Confrontation: When possible, avoid unnecessary confrontation with narcissistic coworkers or superiors. Choose your battles wisely and address issues only when they are critical or essential to your job.

Use Diplomacy: Practice diplomacy and tact when dealing with sensitive topics. Avoid confrontational language and frame your concerns in a professional manner.

Seek Allies: Build alliances with coworkers who may also be dealing with the same narcissistic individual. Having support can help you navigate workplace challenges.

Speak to HR or Management: If the behavior of a narcissistic coworker or superior becomes unbearable, consider speaking to your human resources department or higher management. Provide specific examples and focus on the impact on your work and the overall work environment.

Maintain Professionalism: Regardless of the behavior of narcissistic coworkers or superiors, continue to uphold high standards of professionalism. This can help you stand out as a reliable and competent team member.

Prioritize Self-Care: Outside of work, prioritize self-care and relaxation to help manage the stress of dealing with narcissistic colleagues.

Consider Job Change: If the workplace environment becomes persistently toxic due to narcissistic dynamics and it affects your well-being, it may be worth considering a job change.

Stay Focused on Personal Growth: Focus on your personal and professional growth, setting goals and seeking opportunities for advancement. Your own growth and success can be a powerful counterbalance to workplace challenges.

While dealing with narcissistic individuals in the workplace can be demanding, it's essential to maintain your own well-being and professionalism. By setting boundaries, seeking allies, and considering professional growth, you can navigate these workplace dynamics with greater confidence and resilience.

Chapter 10: Empathy and Compassion

Empathy and compassion are valuable qualities when dealing with narcissistic individuals. In this final chapter, we will discuss the importance of empathy and compassion, and explore the potential for change and growth in people with narcissistic traits.

The Importance of Empathy and Compassion

Promoting Healthy Communication: Empathy allows you to understand the emotions and perspectives of narcissistic individuals. Compassion enables you to respond with kindness and respect. These qualities can promote more effective and constructive communication.

De-escalating Conflicts: Responding to narcissistic behavior with empathy and compassion can help de-escalate conflicts. It reduces the chances of triggering defensive reactions and can lead to a more productive conversation.

Building Connections: Empathy and compassion can create a bridge of understanding between you and the narcissistic individual. This connection can be the foundation for improved interactions and potential growth.

Self-Preservation: While it's important to be empathetic and compassionate, it is equally crucial to protect your own well-being. Setting boundaries and maintaining self-care are integral to ensuring your emotional health.

The Potential for Change and Growth in Narcissistic Individuals

Narcissistic traits exist on a spectrum, and some individuals may be more open to change and growth than others. Here are some factors to consider:

Self-Recognition: Some narcissistic individuals may eventually recognize the negative impact of their behavior on their relationships and well-being. This self-recognition can be a crucial catalyst for change.

Desire for Change: When a narcissistic individual expresses a genuine desire to change, it signals potential for personal growth. They may seek therapy or counseling to work on their behavior.

Therapy and Counseling: Professional therapy can be highly effective in helping narcissistic individuals develop self-awareness, empathy, and healthier interpersonal skills. It can also address any underlying issues that contribute to narcissistic behavior.

Personal Motivation: In some cases, personal motivation and a desire for personal growth can drive a narcissistic individual to actively work on their behavior and relationships.

Slow Progress: Change in narcissistic behavior tends to be gradual and non-linear. It requires patience, both from the individual and those around them.

Acceptance: It's crucial to accept that not all narcissistic individuals are willing or able to change. In such cases, your focus should shift toward self-preservation and maintaining healthy boundaries.

Empathy and compassion can foster change in narcissistic individuals by creating a more supportive and non-confrontational environment. However, it's important to recognize that change is not guaranteed, and your own well-being should always remain a top priority.

As we conclude this book, remember that your journey in dealing with narcissistic individuals is a challenging one, but it offers opportunities for personal growth, self-awareness, and resilience. By employing the strategies and insights discussed throughout this book, you can navigate these complex relationships with greater confidence and well-being.

Potential for Change in the Narcissist

Dealing with a narcissistic individual can be challenging, but it's natural to wonder if change is possible. While narcissistic personality disorder (NPD) is characterized by pervasive patterns of grandiosity, a need for admiration, and a lack of empathy, there is evidence to suggest that some narcissists can experience growth and improvement in their behavior over time. Understanding the potential for change in narcissists and the practical steps that can be taken to facilitate this process is essential for those close to them.

Can Narcissists Change?

The question of whether narcissists can change is complex and multifaceted. While personality disorders such as NPD are considered to be deeply ingrained and resistant to change, research suggests that certain interventions and life experiences can lead to improvements in narcissistic traits. Factors such as motivation for change, self-awareness, and willingness to engage in therapy or self-reflection play a significant role in determining the potential for change in narcissists.

How Can Narcissists Change?

1. **Therapy and Counseling:** Engaging in therapy or counseling with a qualified mental health professional can provide narcissists with the opportunity to explore their thoughts, feelings, and behaviors in a safe and supportive environment.

Therapeutic modalities such as cognitive-behavioral therapy (CBT), psychodynamic therapy, and schema therapy can help narcissists develop insight into the underlying factors driving their behavior and learn healthier coping mechanisms.

2. **Developing Empathy:** Narcissists often struggle with empathy, but through therapy and self-reflection, they can learn to understand and empathize with the experiences and perspectives of others. Techniques such as perspective-taking exercises, role-playing, and guided imagery can help narcissists develop greater empathy and compassion for those around them.

3. **Building Self-Awareness:** Self-awareness is essential for facilitating change in narcissists. By gaining insight into their own thoughts, emotions, and behavior patterns, narcissists can begin to recognize the impact of their actions on others and identify areas for growth and improvement. Journaling, mindfulness practices, and feedback from trusted individuals can help narcissists develop greater self-awareness and insight.

4. **Setting Boundaries:** Those close to narcissists can play a crucial role in facilitating change by setting and enforcing healthy boundaries. Clearly communicating expectations, expressing concerns about problematic behavior, and refusing to enable or condone narcissistic behavior can help create accountability and encourage narcissists to consider the impact of their actions on others.

5. **Encouraging Self-Reflection:** Encouraging narcissists to engage in self-reflection and introspection can help foster personal growth and development. Asking open-ended questions, providing constructive feedback, and expressing empathy and understanding can create opportunities for narcissists to examine their thoughts, feelings, and motivations more deeply.

6. **Modeling Healthy Behavior:** Modeling healthy behavior and communication can provide narcissists with positive examples to emulate. Demonstrating empathy, active listening, and assertive communication skills can help narcissists learn new ways of relating to others and expressing themselves more effectively.

Practical Steps for Implementing Change:

1. **Express Concerns:** Express your concerns about the impact of the narcissist's behavior on yourself and others in a non-confrontational and empathetic manner. Focus on how their behavior affects you personally and avoid blaming or criticizing them.

2. **Encourage Therapy:** Encourage the narcissist to seek therapy or counseling with a qualified mental health professional who specializes in treating personality disorders. Offer your support and encouragement throughout the process, emphasizing the potential benefits of therapy for personal growth and improvement.

3. **Set Boundaries:** Set and enforce healthy boundaries with the narcissist to protect your own well-being and encourage accountability. Clearly communicate your expectations and consequences for violating boundaries, and be prepared to follow through with consequences if necessary.

4. **Provide Feedback:** Provide constructive feedback to the narcissist about their behavior, focusing on specific examples and the impact it has on you and others. Use "I" statements to express your feelings and observations, and avoid making generalizations or assumptions about their intentions.

5. **Practice Empathy:** Practice empathy and understanding towards the narcissist, recognizing that their behavior may be driven by underlying insecurities or past experiences. Validate their feelings and experiences while also holding them accountable for their actions.

6. **Seek Support:** Seek support from friends, family, or a therapist to navigate your relationship with the narcissist and cope with the challenges it presents. Surround yourself with individuals who understand your situation and can offer validation, empathy, and practical advice.

While change is possible for some narcissists, it requires a combination of self-awareness, motivation, and external support.

By encouraging therapy, setting boundaries, providing feedback, practicing empathy, and seeking support, those close to narcissists can play a crucial role in facilitating personal growth and improvement. However, it's essential to recognize that change may be slow and incremental, and not all narcissists may be willing or able to engage in the process of change.

<u>Chapter 11: Moving Forward</u>

As we come to the end of this book, it's essential to reflect on the key takeaways and recognize the importance of self-awareness and self-care in dealing with narcissistic individuals. In this final chapter, we will summarize the critical lessons learned and encourage readers to apply what they've learned in their relationships and personal growth.

Key Takeaways

Understanding Narcissism: Narcissism is a complex personality trait that exists on a spectrum. It can range from healthy self-esteem to narcissistic personality disorder (NPD).

Recognizing Narcissistic Behavior: Narcissistic behavior is characterized by a lack of empathy, an exaggerated sense of self-importance, a constant need for admiration, and a sense of entitlement.

Impact on Relationships: Narcissistic behavior can have a profound impact on relationships, leading to conflicts, emotional distress, and a sense of powerlessness.

Setting Boundaries: Establishing and maintaining clear boundaries is vital when dealing with narcissistic individuals. Boundaries help protect your emotional well-being.

Self-Care: Prioritizing self-care, both physical and emotional, is essential for maintaining your well-being in relationships affected by narcissistic behavior.

Building Resilience: Building emotional resilience allows you to bounce back from adversity and maintain your emotional well-being.

Empathy and Compassion: Responding to narcissistic behavior with empathy and compassion can promote healthier communication and potentially foster change in individuals with narcissistic traits.

The Importance of Self-Awareness and Self-Care

Self-awareness is the foundation of personal growth and well-being. By understanding your own needs, values, and boundaries, you can navigate relationships with narcissistic individuals more effectively. Self-awareness also allows you to recognize the impact of narcissistic behavior on your emotional and psychological health.

Self-care is the practice of taking deliberate steps to maintain and improve your well-being. It's not a selfish act but a necessary one for safeguarding your emotional health. Self-care encompasses physical, emotional, and psychological aspects, including setting boundaries, practicing self-compassion, and seeking support when needed.

Applying What You've Learned

Now that you've gained valuable insights and strategies for dealing with narcissistic individuals, it's time to apply what you've learned in your relationships and personal growth:

Set and Maintain Boundaries: Continue to establish and enforce clear boundaries in your relationships to protect your well-being.

Practice Self-Care: Prioritize self-care to ensure that your physical and emotional needs are met. This will help you build resilience and maintain a balanced perspective.

Seek Support: Lean on your support network when needed. Sharing your experiences and feelings with trusted friends, family, or a therapist can be invaluable.

Build Emotional Resilience: Work on building your emotional resilience to bounce back from adversity and maintain your emotional well-being.

Show Empathy and Compassion: Approach your interactions with narcissistic individuals with empathy and compassion when appropriate. This can promote more productive communication and possibly encourage positive change.

Personal Growth: Focus on your personal growth, setting goals and seeking opportunities for advancement in your personal and professional life.

Remember that your journey in dealing with narcissistic individuals is a challenging but transformative one. By implementing the strategies and insights discussed in this book, you can navigate these complex relationships with greater confidence and well-being. As you move forward, prioritize your emotional health, continue to learn and grow, and nurture the relationships that truly enhance your life.

<u>**Conclusion: A Journey of Understanding and Empowerment**</u>

In our exploration of narcissistic traits and the complexities of navigating relationships with narcissistic individuals, we've delved into a world that can be challenging, emotionally taxing, and at times, bewildering. However, it's crucial to remember that this journey is also one of profound understanding and empowerment.

The Significance of Understanding and Managing Narcissistic Traits

Understanding and managing narcissistic traits are vital for several reasons. First and foremost, it allows us to protect our emotional and psychological well-being in the face of behavior that can be manipulative, draining, and harmful. By recognizing narcissistic behavior and setting clear boundaries, we create a shield of self-preservation that allows us to maintain our own sense of self-worth and peace of mind.

Furthermore, understanding narcissistic traits can help us navigate these complex relationships with more empathy and compassion. It enables us to communicate effectively, potentially fostering growth and change in individuals who exhibit narcissistic behavior.

A Message of Hope and Empowerment

As we conclude this journey, it's important to emphasize that there is hope and empowerment to be found in dealing with narcissistic individuals. You have learned valuable strategies, insights, and tools to protect your well-being, build resilience, and promote healthier interactions. You possess the strength and wisdom to apply these lessons in your life.

While change in narcissistic individuals may be gradual and non-linear, it is possible. Some individuals may come to recognize the negative impact of their behavior and seek personal growth and transformation. By responding with empathy and compassion when appropriate, you can play a role in fostering change.

Your Action Plan

To empower you in your ongoing journey, consider the following action plan:

Reflect on Your Own Well-being: Regularly assess your emotional health and well-being. Understand the impact of your interactions with narcissistic individuals on your life.

Set and Maintain Boundaries: Continue to establish and enforce clear boundaries in your relationships, focusing on self-preservation.

Prioritize Self-Care: Make self-care a non-negotiable priority. Ensure that your physical and emotional needs are met, and practice self-compassion.

Build Resilience: Work on building your emotional resilience to bounce back from adversity and maintain your emotional well-being.

Show Empathy and Compassion: Approach interactions with narcissistic individuals with empathy and compassion when appropriate, promoting productive communication.

Focus on Personal Growth: Set goals and seek opportunities for personal and professional growth. Continue to learn and grow, using your experiences to shape a brighter future.

Remember that your journey is one of transformation and self-discovery. It is an opportunity to build resilience, set healthier boundaries, and find strength in the face of challenges. As you move forward, prioritize your well-being, maintain a sense of hope, and foster positive change in your relationships. You have the power to navigate these complexities with grace, empathy, and the wisdom gained from this journey.